POSTED
NO TRESPASSING

YOUR GUIDE TO GAINING PERMISSION TO HUNT ON PRIVATE PROPERTY

By

Brian Guerro

ISBN: 1-4107-6085-5 (e-book)
ISBN: 1-4107-6084-7 (Paperback)

This book is printed on acid free paper.

1stBooks – rev. 06/16/03

ACKNOWLEDGEMENTS

I dedicate this book to my sons. I hope that with the help of this book, the tradition of hunting will be preserved for their children.

I would like to thank my parents. Throughout my life they have provided me with an environment of love and encouragement.

I want to thank my Uncle Vince for the very special memories. He took me deer hunting when my father had to work. Coincidentally, on both of these occasions, I got a buck.

Thank you to Kirk Zucal, a friend who introduced me to hunting with a bow and a muzzleloader. While growing up, he unknowingly served as a mentor for me to follow on hunting adventures.

A very special thank you to Alex Cortezzo who has granted me and my family permission to hunt on his property for so many years – thanks for the great memories.

I want to give special thanks to Melanie Gold, Kay Bond, Fran Hoffman and Scott Mulitch for their thoughts and encouragement.

TABLE OF CONTENTS

PURPOSE

Hunting is becoming an endangered tradition in our modern times. Fewer people partake in the sport as the amount of huntable land decreases year after year. Many hunters become frustrated because they are being squeezed onto smaller parcels of land and eventually give up hunting completely. Public use lands such as state owned forests and game lands become overcrowded as development encroaches on privately owned land. The privately owned wilderness areas that remain are most likely **"POSTED"**.

In addition to providing you with information on how to gain access to private property, this guide is written with the underlying purpose of promoting hunter-landowner relations. In order to preserve the tradition of hunting and to pass it on to future generations, we must remember to respect not only the game we pursue but the land and its owner as well.

It is the purpose of this guide to provide you with information and suggestions on how to gain access to those properties marked **"POSTED – NO TRESPASSING."** Whether you've lost your old hunting grounds to development or have just been eyeing some property where you know you'll find "Mr. Big," this book will provide you with the ammunition to target the owners of those **"NO TRESPASSING"** signs and get their permission to allow you access to the land.

You will learn about ways to investigate the property and the property owner. You will read about different strategies to use in approaching the landowner. I discuss topics such as leases, insurance and hunting clubs. Samples of advertisements, letters and conversations are provided to help you successfully present yourself to encourage the landowner to say "Yes!" to your request.

x

INTRODUCTION

I didn't think it would happen to me, but it did. The land I used to hunt was now filled with big, yellow earth-moving equipment and partially built houses. Imagine the place where you grew up hunting; where you shot your first buck and have memories of autumn days with friends and family. Now your favorite spot is part of someone's back yard. Imagine the developer had the gall to name one of the roads in the new development 'Hunter Lane'.

I looked on the bright side. This would help to funnel the deer into another area I knew pretty well. While scouting the new area one spring day it happened again. The earthmovers were back. This time to build a shopping center. Now what do I do? Give up hunting?

Wow! What a nightmare! That was what I thought as I woke up early that morning on the first day of bow season. The thought of not having a place to hunt quickly slipped my mind as I hurried to get my equipment together and head out to the spot that had been my favorite for the past 24 years. As I turned onto the road, the flash of the "NO TRESPASSING" signs that I helped put up shone from the glare of my headlights as I drove by. I pulled up to the spot where my family and I have parked for years, my truck's grille a mere six feet away from a "NO TRESPASSING" sign. I sat in the truck and sipped some coffee staring at the "NO TRESPASSING" sign. My mind drifted away from the anticipation of the hunt. I wondered, "What if I didn't know the person who's signature was on that sign"? The thought stayed with me as I ascended to my stand and throughout the morning. As I walked back to my truck later that day, I decided to put more thought into what would happen if, in fact, that scenario were true.

I never bothered to think about it before. I'd taken advantage of the privilege of hunting private property because the landowner is a friend of the family. I assumed I'd always have permission to hunt these lands. I would hunt on state game lands but my recollection was of people walking in at first light and making all kinds of noise. It was bad enough to have someone posted 50 yards away from me, but one morning as I approached my stand there was already someone sitting in it.

I decided to set out on a new hunting expedition: to search for a successful way to gain permission to hunt on private property. You are holding the results of this search in your hands.

For reference purposes, this guide relates primarily to deer hunting, but the concepts can be used in any situation. Simply put, this guide will help you to identify a property owner through one or more of many methods. Then you use the suggestions for approaching landowners and convince them to agree to your request for permission to hunt on their land. For brevity, I will refer to the landowner in masculine form, but keep in mind that the landowner could easily be a female.

CHAPTER 1

THE SCOUTING BEGINS

The first step in scouting for permission to hunt on private property is to figure out what kind of hunting you plan on doing. For example, if you are primarily a pheasant hunter you wouldn't want to spend your time trying to get permission to hunt on someone's property which is mainly hardwoods.

The second step is to seek out the property or properties you want to hunt on. You may have a specific piece of property in mind or you may be open to a totally new location. Maybe you've seen deer cross the road in the same place every morning on your way to work. Perhaps everyone has been talking about a big buck that has been spotted in a farmer's field. Maybe there's a private piece of property that borders a game preserve. Whatever it is, keep in mind that just because the land is marked "POSTED – NO TRESPASSING" or "NO HUNTING", the primary reason the landowner put up those signs is to protect himself legally. It doesn't mean that he will automatically deny you permission.

Once you have found some property you would like to hunt on, the next step is to look at some maps. Both topographical maps and conventional road maps are very useful. The topographical maps will help with terrain: fields, valleys, mountains, creeks, etc. The road maps will help to narrow down the exact location of the property within the county, township or borough.

When you have located the property you wish to hunt on and located the county or township it lies in, the next step is to find out who owns it. Now, this could be a business, a farmer or a private individual. Whoever it is, you're going to have to do some investigating. This may not come easy. I suggest you not put all of your eggs in one basket and, instead, investigate a number of properties at the same time. This could be beneficial in many ways.

First, it will save you time since you will be using many of the same methods to research each property. Second, because deer and other game travel from one property to another, it would be to your advantage to be able to have permission to cross those "NO TRESPASSING" signs in between properties. Third, sometimes one landowner may be reluctant to give you permission until he finds out that the guy down the road lets you hunt his property.

Now you will need to do a little detective work. Here are several methods you might use to track down the owner of a specific piece of property. If one doesn't work, try another or a combination of them.

Observation

You can first look for the obvious. If there is a house nearby and you suspect the property owner lives there, look for the name on the mailbox. Write it down along with the address. Don't forget to check for a signature on the "NO TRESPASSING" sign if there is one. If you know the street address you can go to a library and find *"The Blue Book" Cross-Reference Directory*. It is published by City Publishing Company, Inc. in Independence, KS. This directory lists people by their addresses (city, street) instead of alphabetically by name.

You may be lucky enough to spot a neighborly looking person nearby. You could drive by and ask him or her who owns the property you're looking at. If there is no one available to ask, you might try finding the name or address on the nearest mailbox as a starting reference point. This information will be helpful when referencing tax maps in the local courthouse records office.

Records Office

The local records office and tax assessment office are places you will want to get familiar with. These two offices hold a wealth of information about properties and their owners in your county and it's all free, public access information.

Once you have some information about a property owner such as his name or address, you should verify that the person you are going to contact is, in fact, the owner of the property. The records office and tax assessment office in that particular county keeps files about the property and the landowner in books, on computer or on microfilm.

There are instructions available at the office that will guide you and there is usually a friendly clerk that can help you. Once you learn how to use the system you should be able to look up the maps of the property, acreage, owner's name, address, county and township. You can use the information to compare to your road map and topographical map to verify that this is the property you'd like to hunt on. If you used the suggestion above and wrote down the name and address from the nearest mailbox, you can use the tax map of that property to find adjacent properties. Once you have found the information you need, most offices have a printer or a copier that you can use to make copies of the information.

Don't feel uncomfortable about using the information at these offices. It is there for public use. There are plenty of people who access this information every day like bankers, Realtors and attorneys. So that you don't feel out of place, I suggest that you wear something casual but appropriate to the environment. Don't visit these offices dressed in your hunting garb. Save that for the woods.

The records and tax assessment offices are government run and follow the hours of a typical government office so you may have to take some time off from work one day to do your investigating. To maximize your time and effort, be prepared to look up several properties during your visit. There is a chance that the preliminary information you've collected for a specific property is not correct and you will not be able to complete your search. If you are prepared to look up several properties, you can simply go on to investigate the next property on your list. Also, there is no guarantee that the landowner of one particular property will grant you permission to hunt. If your request is rejected by one landowner, you already have the necessary information from the records office to go on to pursue permission from another property owner.

Internet

Another useful way to research property is with the use of a computer through the Internet. There are many ways to search for names and addresses. In most cases all you need to do is type in someone's name and the computer will give you their complete address and sometimes a phone number too. Or, you could type in the address and the computer will search to match it to a name. If it is a farm you are targeting, your state agricultural department may have a web page on the Internet which could provide you with general information about farms in your area.

If you don't have a computer, your nearest public library probably has computers with Internet access that you can use – and in some cases you can use them for free. Also, local colleges have computers that you may be able to use. Don't forget to ask friends or relatives who own computers if you can do some work on the Internet if they have access.

You can also search the Internet for maps. The Internet has special pages where you need only to enter an address and the computer will produce a map of the area.

Wildlife Agencies

If you don't have a specific piece of property in mind, wildlife agencies may be very useful. Wildlife agencies can be organized on the local, regional or state level. They may point you in the direction of property owners who, when asked, regularly allow hunters on their property. They may also have information or lists of farmers who have complained about crop damage. Some states allow liberal hunting in these areas with the agreement that the farmer will allow hunters access.

The wildlife agencies may also provide you with deer density and road kill statistics in the area you're interested in. Try to get as much information as possible from the wildlife agent, like names and addresses to make your job easier. If all you get is the name of a road with high road kill occurrences, then follow the previous steps to help you locate the name and address of landowners on that road.

You may find that no single method will provide you with 100% of the results you want. In fact, a combination of them, depending on your situation, will probably work best. Practice makes perfect, so be sure to make notes for yourself about what works and what doesn't. It will make your research easier in the future.

Let's assume you have found out who owns the property you want to hunt on. What do you do next? In the next chapter, read about the various approaches and techniques you can use to contact the landowner once you have identified him.

CHAPTER 2

STRATEGY AND APPROACH

Specific Properties

When planning a hunt, you develop a specific strategy. You plan what time you will enter the hunting area, which weapon you will use, what supplies you will bring, what you will wear and so on. You prepare yourself through research and planning ahead. When you set out on your hunt for permission to access private property, you must plan a similar strategy.

This chapter discusses strategies to use when approaching the owner of a specific piece of property you want to hunt on. I have categorized these landowners into three different groups: farmers, private individuals and businesses. Chapter 3 will discuss strategies to use to get permission to hunt on nonspecific land.

You know exactly where you want to hunt and you have learned who owns it. Now you may be apprehensive about pulling into this person's driveway, walking up to the door, knocking and asking for permission to hunt on his property.

Believe me, I know the feeling of not knowing who you are going to meet or what his reaction might be. That's why it is best to write a letter to the landowner first to explain who you are and what your interests are. A letter is the most non-intrusive approach and allows the landowner to become familiar with you and to consider your request without pressure and without feeling awkward. You'll probably be much more relaxed later when you have the opportunity to talk face-to-face with the landowner knowing that he is prepared to listen to your request and has some idea of who you are. A letter allows you to make your first contact with the landowner without interrupting their daily lives. Think about how it makes you feel when telemarketers interrupt you on the telephone or door-to-door salesmen interrupt you at your door. Now think about how you would feel if some stranger walked up to your door without warning and asked if he could walk around your yard with a high-powered weapon to hunt animals.

Whether the landowner is a farmer, private individual or a business, this section provides information on how to prepare to meet these landowners face-to-face. The sample letters, found in the Appendix, conclude by giving the landowner the opportunity to contact you to arrange a meeting. When writing the letter, correct spelling of the landowner's name and a professional appearance are important.

The letter and envelope should be neatly typed and your return address should be on both of them. You may also consider enclosing a self-addressed, stamped envelope. You may want to include a personal profile, references, a reply slip and possibly a lease worksheet with the introduction letter. All of these items are explained in later chapters. Examples of these can be found in the Appendix.

Approaching Farmers

So, you sent a letter to a farmer and he responded by calling you. You spoke with him briefly by phone and arranged a time to meet. Now you need to ask yourself, "What do I know about this farmer that can put some common ground between us and make our meeting more relaxed?"

You know the farmer lives at the place where he works. His livelihood is tied to his land. He endures the extremes of Mother Nature and the uncertainty of the commodities market. His land is the first thing he sees when he wakes up in the morning and the last thing he sees when he goes to sleep at night. When something breaks it's his problem, not the maintenance department's. When he goes to sell his crops it is his problem, not the sales department's. A farmer is like a one-man company. The life of a farmer is very different than the life of most people. You need to find some common ground to show the farmer that you understand and respect his way of life.

To accomplish this, do a little research before you contact him. The farmer doesn't want to hear just about you and what a great hunter you are and how much you want to hunt on his property. By knowing about the farmer and what he does, you will be able to engage in intelligent conversation with him. He will be pleased to hear about your interest in his business and not just in his land and the game that it may hold. Your knowledge and interest in what the farmer does will show your respect for him and he will naturally have more respect for you.

To help you prepare for your meeting with a farmer, the following list contains some questions that you may want to consider about him and some possible ways to engage in conversation to get you started. Some of this information could be gathered by taking a slow ride by the prospective farm.

▸ What kind of tractor does the farmer have?
   Example: John Deere, Case, New Holland
   You could go to a local dealer or farm show and get some information on the type of tractor that the farmer has. Learn if it is for plowing or no-till farming.

▸ What type of grains does this type of tractor pick?
   Example: Corn, Soybeans, Wheat
   The farmer might be very impressed to hear you say, "I hear those New Holland's are the best tractors you can buy for picking soy beans. Is that true?"

▸ Does the farmer have orchards?
   Example: Apples, Pears, Peaches
   You will most certainly please the farmer when you say something like, "I understand it's very hard work to keep a peach orchard productive. How do you do it?"

▸ What kind of crops does the farmer raise?
> *Example: Corn, Soybeans, Hay, Wheat, Oats, Vegetables*
> You can ask the farmer if he sells to any local markets or to the public. If he raises hay, ask him if it's alfalfa or timothy. Ask him what the difference is between them.

▸ How has the weather been to the farmer?
> *Example: Has there been a drought recently? Has there been too much rain? Was the winter longer than usual? Was there early or late frost?*
> The weather is one of the farmer's greatest friends and foes and he will surely realize that you are in tune with his way of life by asking how the weather has affected him.

▸ What kind of animals does the farmer raise?
> *Example: Cows, Chickens, Pigs, Horses*
> Ask him if he's ever kept any other kind of animal. Which is the hardest one to raise?

▸ What kind of truck does the farmer have?
> *Example: Ford, Chevy, Dodge*
> Perhaps you have or had a similar truck and you can discuss how much you liked it.

Some other topics that will interest the farmer are things like the Environmental Protection Agency. They are always knocking on the farmer's door and coming up with new research about the effects of pesticides, fertilizers and herbicides. Have you read anything in the newspaper or heard anything on the news lately about these topics?

It's easy to pick up monthly farming industry magazines or newspapers to familiarize yourself with the concerns of the farmer. Your state agriculture department is another source of information about farming. Many states have a web page on the Internet where you can find loads of information including facts about farming, publications, news releases and market reports. This will enable you to talk to the farmer about other issues besides your own personal interests.

It is equally important to keep in mind some things that you should not do:

▸ Do not drink, smoke or chew tobacco
▸ Do not bring your friends
▸ Do not wear your camouflage or anything orange
▸ Do not wear a suit
▸ Do not bring your young children

Time of year

Now that you know a little bit about the farmer, you need to plan your strategy regarding the time of the year that you will approach him to request his permission to hunt on his land. You want to approach the farmer at a time when he is least stressed and most willing to listen to your proposal. One thing is for certain. It would be inappropriate to ask permission of anyone to hunt two days before the season opener.

From your research you should have learned what type of farming the landowner is engaged in. This may depend on what part of the country you live in. The growing periods for crop farmers are determined by the change of the seasons and the weather. It is wisest not to approach a crop farmer during the busy planting or harvesting times. However, for the livestock farmer, every season is busy. That's why sending a letter first is so important. It gives the farmer the opportunity to prepare to meet with you and he can decide on a convenient time.

The chart on page 59 shows a typical farming schedule. Use this chart as a starting point to find out when the farmer in your area is likely to be least stressed and more willing to listen to your request for permission to hunt on his property. If he is busy planting or harvesting crops, he may not be interested in listening to your request to use his land for your recreation.

The chart is generalized and doesn't reflect any unusual weather conditions, regional planting and harvesting times, mechanical difficulties in their equipment or medical crises. Be observant of the elements that effect the farmer. Extreme weather conditions such as freezing temperatures, drought or floods effect all farmers.

Any time of the year may work for you depending on the individual farmer, but putting some consideration into your approach and selecting a time when the farmer is least stressed may greatly enhance your chances of obtaining permission to hunt.

Approaching Private Individuals (Non-Farmers)

When approaching someone who doesn't farm but owns a huntable piece of property, the time of year may not be so critical. However, I would still refrain from asking for permission to hunt just prior to or during the hunting season. Also, to prepare the landowner for your request, it is best to contact him first by writing a letter and then by arranging a face-to-face meeting.

The property owner may be someone who has never hunted before. He may be someone who decided to take his high income and buy a piece of prime real estate in the country. He may be a small-property owner with access to prime hunting grounds. There is plenty of good hunting in small pockets of wooded lots and on the fringes of housing developments. These areas can hold huge bucks.

Some people may be anti-hunting or anti-gun and be very passionate about their beliefs. Expect to meet some resistance. Probably most important to a landowner is feeling secure. It will be your job to convince him that you are not a threat to his family, property, or pets and that you are a responsible, law abiding, ethical hunter.

Another concern for a property owner is shot placement. Know the safety zone limits of your state. Let the property owner know the safety zone limits too. They will undoubtedly feel a bit more comfortable knowing that you are informed of the laws and have taken the very important aspect of their safety into consideration. Small wooded lots may be too close to homes or roads to ensure safety. Perhaps you could bow hunt in this area if you're within the safety zone limits and it is legal in your state. In my state, the safety zone for both bow and rifle is 150 yards, but I still wouldn't feel comfortable sitting on a stand with my rifle and be able to see houses in the distance. This may be a 'bow only' location just by your own safety standards. If you are planning to contact a landowner in this type of area, consider the fact that it may not be huntable if you don't plan on using a bow. A quick determination on your part may save a waste of your time.

One more thing to consider before you contact the private landowner is the route you need to take to access the land you wish to hunt. Look at a topographical map of the area to analyze the property for its accessibility. Because the property may be relatively small, you need to think about your morning or afternoon approach to your stand. Will you have to walk across a field or through the landowner's yard to access the woods? Will you need to walk in from the back of a shopping center? Where will you park your truck or car? Be ready to tell the landowner of your plan. They will appreciate that you took the time to consider things like not disturbing them at 4:00 in the morning or not parking in their driveway so that they can get their own cars out.

Before approaching a private landowner, you should find out a few things about him to drum up conversation when you meet. The list of questions to ask yourself may not be as long and complex as that for the farmer, but they are equally important.

Take note of these simple things:

- ▸ What kinds of car(s) are parked outside?
- ▸ Are there any pets? Look for a dog chain or doghouse.
- ▸ Are there any kids? Look for bikes, swingsets and toys.
- ▸ What kind of lawn mower does he have?
- ▸ Is there a flower or vegetable garden that you can talk about?
- ▸ Is there an old or unique car that could start conversation?
- ▸ Are there any signs of new construction?

You don't want the general non-farming landowner to think you know too much about him or he will become suspicious and uncomfortable, thinking that you have been stalking him or scoping out his house for a robbery. Keep the conversation light and limited to those things that are easily visible.

Before meeting with the landowner, realize that the landowner's first impression of you will be based on your appearance as well as how you present yourself. Dress up a little; not in a suit and a tie but wear a nice button-down shirt and a clean pair of jeans and clean shoes. Dressing nicely will help the landowner to see you as his equal and can only weigh favorably for you.

Whatever you choose to wear, do yourself and everyone else a favor, to improve our image as hunters; don't wear your camouflage or your fluorescent orange. Another word of caution: the landowner doesn't need to know how successful a hunter you are, so spare him from all the gory details of your success.

Remember to be patient regardless of who you are approaching for permission. Sometimes a landowner doesn't want to make a commitment for a long period of time. Ask if you can just hunt during bow season or for small game on a Saturday.

Once you are granted permission, remember to strictly abide by the rules that you agreed upon with the landowner. If you said you would hunt only doe, you'd better be dragging a tagged doe to your truck. If you said you would be hunting with one friend, there better be only two of you entering and leaving the property.

Also, don't think your job is done after you get permission to hunt. You need to build a relationship with the landowner. Stop in and visit every so often to say "hello" or maybe bring something like vegetables from your garden or some homemade baked goods. See more on building this friendship in Chapter 5; Nurturing the Relationship.

Approaching Businesses

Many businesses – whether large or small – may own prime, huntable land. It may be easier to break into Fort Knox than to get permission to hunt on these properties, but it's not impossible.

Dealing with businesses will require more research, professionalism, selling, and patience than dealing with a farmer or private individual. For these reasons, there are not a lot of people knocking down the doors of businesses to ask for hunting permission. In fact, businesses are probably the last landowners most hunters will seek out for permission to hunt.

Research

Let's assume you know the name of the business that owns the property you wish to hunt on. You may have learned this from any one of the techniques described in Chapter 1. More research is now required to seek out the individual or individuals that have the authority to grant you the permission you want.

One thing that would definitely make your task easier is knowing someone who works for the business. Simply explain what your intentions are and ask your contact to find out who you need to write to.

If you don't know someone 'on the inside' you could try contacting the business by telephone. You need to be careful here. You may not want to disclose exactly what your intentions are until you've connected with whoever has the authority to grant or decline permission.

Keep in mind that local offices may not employ the people who have the authority to grant hunting privileges. They may just be a small group of employees. Some of them may even hunt on the property themselves without anyone in the corporation knowing it. Now, if you were the one with 'exclusive' hunting privileges, are you going to volunteer the name, address and phone number of the person in charge? Probably not.

The Right Person

The person you need to contact may be in the regional office or the corporate office. If the business is publicly owned, the library is the place to go to learn the name of the people in charge. Reference books such as Dun & Bradstreet, Ward's Business Directory of U.S. Private and Public Companies and Standard & Poors provide information about publicly owned companies. From these books you can find the names and job titles of the people in charge.

Let's say you've been very successful and found the names of three possible people with the authority to grant permission: the president, vice president and CEO. To whom should you address the letter? That's easy. Send a letter to each of them. You see, chances are that none of these people will even see your letter.

Your letter will probably be opened, read and then forwarded by a secretary or an assistant to whom they believe is the appropriate person to respond to your letter. By sending more than one letter you are increasing your chances that it will get read by the right person. This could be the manager of facility services, maintenance or public affairs, to name a few. You see, with businesses structured in so many different ways, it's extremely difficult as an outsider to know EXACTLY who to send a letter to on the first try. Before you send your letter out, let's consider some other things.

Professionalism

By being professional, you will present yourself in a manner similar to that of the person you are dealing with. We assume that a person with the authority to grant (or deny) you the permission to hunt on the company property will act in a business like fashion. They will dress and speak in a business like manner. They will expect the same from you. Your correspondence with this person should be neatly typed and correctly spelled and follow a business format. When you have the opportunity to meet with this person, you should dress appropriately and speak as you would if you were having a job interview with him or her. Be clear, concise and know what you are talking about.

Selling

To win the favor of a business owner or executive, you may have to do a little more selling and be more persuasive than you are accustomed to. Business owners and executives are busy people. They don't usually allow much time for things that aren't going to help their business or their career. Unlike the farmer, they're accustomed to interacting with salesmen and the salesman approach rather than a couple of 'good old boys' looking for a place to hunt.

Your first contact with this person should be by letter. This letter will make the first impression on the permission giver. Remember to keep it brief (not more than one page) and professional (a business format, typed and spelled correctly). The letter has to 'sell' your request to the permission giver – enough to encourage them to want to speak with you in more detail. You may want to prepare yourself even before you send the letter by reading some books on selling such as, "How to Sell Yourself" by Joe Girard or "Say It Right, How to Talk in Any Business Situation" by Lillian Glass, Ph.D.

A sample of an introduction letter is included in the Appendix and it should include:

- ▸ Who you are
- ▸ Why you are contacting them
- ▸ Profile of the individual or hunting club

▸ References (such as other properties the individual or club has permission to hunt on)
▸ Reply slip and self-addressed stamped envelope

If, after sending the letter, you have the opportunity to meet with the person, you should consider some of the following things:

▸ You may offer to take him or her to lunch. If he or she accepts:
  − A few days before the meeting, find a restaurant close to the business. If you don't know of any, ask him or her to suggest a place.
  − Take a drive to the place of business and the restaurant to determine how long it will take you to get there.
  − Plan to spend no more than 1 hour at lunch.
  − Plan to pay for lunch.
  − If all you have to drive is a beat-up pick-up truck, find alternative transportation.

▸ Don't be late. Be about 10 minutes early. Wait in the parking lot if you arrive too early.

▸ If appropriate, wear a suit and tie.

▸ Keep the conversation light and stick to subjects such as what the company does and don't dive right into your interest in hunting on the property.

▸ Bring a small briefcase or portfolio with extra copies of the following:
  − Club or individual profile
  − Insurance information
  − Lease Worksheet

▸ Don't tell hunting stories unless you're asked. You may be lucky enough that the businessperson is a hunter too.

Other things to consider before contacting a company are:

▸ If you are representing a hunting club, will the land support the number of hunters in your club? Explain that the club has other properties and the members of the club draw straws so that not too many hunters are at one location at the same time.

▸ Will the club be hunting during working hours or only on weekends? Are employees working on weekends?

▸ Do employees of the company hunt on the property?

Persistence

As I mentioned at the beginning of this section, breaking into Fort Knox may be easier than getting permission to hunt on property owned by a business. To be successful, you will need to be persistent.

Don't be discouraged if you get no response from the first letter you send. Send another. You may choose to keep the same wording or change it a bit. You may choose to send it to the same person or do a little more research and get the name of someone else to send it to.

If, after sending several letters, you are still unsuccessful, you can try contacting the businessperson by phone. Be prepared to be quick and to the point. Let the businessperson know that you understand he or she is very busy and would like only 5 minutes of his or her time. Explain who you are and that you have sent several letters seeking permission to hunt on the business' property. Tell the businessperson that you are anxious for their reply and that you would like to meet with him or her in three days or at his or her convenience. For example, if you call on Monday, tell the businessperson that you can stop in on Thursday. Suggest discussing your business over lunch.

If you are still unsuccessful, take all that you have learned and move on to the next company. Know the difference between persistence and beating a dead horse. Use all your resources and experience to get the end result you desire. If not at ABC Company, then maybe at XYZ Company.

CHAPTER 3

STRATEGY AND APPROACH

Nonspecific Properties & Reluctant Landowners

This section provides some ideas on how to put the odds in your favor when you don't have a specific piece of property in mind to hunt on or you've been turned down by a reluctant landowner.

This chapter is broken down into three sections. "Tax Time" is about presenting your request for permission to hunt on private property at the same time tax notices are issued to landowners. "Land for Sale" discusses the benefits of seeking permission to hunt on land that is for sale. The final section, "Bulletin Boards", is about strategically advertising your desire to seek permission to hunt on private land.

Note that these three strategies may be more effective if you are willing to pay for hunting privileges in the form of a lease. Leasing is discussed in detail in Chapter 7.

Tax Time

Getting permission to hunt on private property may be more successful if tackled at the right time of year. I am talking about tax time. There is something provoking about receiving tax notices in the mail. People get upset about paying taxes for a variety of reasons, and sometimes it's hard to see exactly what you're paying for.

Remember the guy who denied you permission to hunt on his land four months ago? He may be willing to reevaluate his decision now. Around the same time the county, school or local taxes are sent out, write him a letter indicating that you are still interested in gaining permission to hunt on his land and would be willing to pay for this privilege. Note that this technique could also be used for a landowner you have never contacted before. By sending your letter at the same time the taxes are sent, the landowner will have his tax notice in one hand and your letter proposing to help pay his taxes in the other hand. The landowner may be more receptive to giving you permission to hunt on his property in exchange for money.

You could even find out what the landowner's tax assessment is through tax records at the county records office. This would give you an idea of how much to offer for the lease. If you don't know when a certain tax comes out in a specific area, find out the county name and then contact the county tax office.

Delinquent Taxes

Landowners who have not paid their taxes on time may be even more receptive to your offer to lease their land for hunting privileges. When taxes are delinquent, tax collection notices are sent to the property owners. Additionally, the property owner's name and address may be posted in the local newspaper. This is the tax collector's way of getting the delinquent landowner's attention. These notices are usually printed once a year depending on the community. This is a great time to approach the reluctant landowner with your win-win proposal: the landowner's taxes get paid and you get hunting privileges.

You can call the local tax collector to find out when the notices for delinquent taxes will be sent out and at what time they will be posted in the newspaper. The newspaper usually lists the property owner's names in alphabetical order and includes the address and how much tax each landowner's owes. By looking at the amount of the delinquent taxes, you can discern which properties are small and which are large. Obviously, a person with a large piece of property is going to pay more taxes than someone with a small residential lot with an average house on it.

If you're approaching landowners solely based on delinquent tax notices in the newspaper, you should get out your road maps, topographical maps and tax maps. Find out where the property is located and determine where there might be good hunting opportunities. From tax maps you should be able to find out how much property the landowner owns and the boundaries. The topographical maps will help you to determine the terrain of the property. The road maps will help you to locate the property. Take a ride by the land to determine how it looks first-hand. If the property meets your expectations, it's time to approach the landowner.

You should now have all the information you need to write a letter to the landowner. You have his name, address and how much property he owns. You have an idea of what the terrain is like and you're pretty sure you would like to hunt there. You also know the landowner could be motivated to grant hunting privileges to satisfy his tax obligation.

It's time to whip up a letter and send it out. You may only have six months or so from the time a delinquent tax notice is posted until there is a sheriff's sale – depending on your state.

You will find examples of letters in the Appendix that you can use to approach a landowner at tax time. Remember that your letter must have correct spelling and a professional appearance. The letter and envelope should be neatly typed and your return address should be on both the letter and the envelope. You may want to include the following information with the introduction letter:

- ▸ Personal or club profile
- ▸ References
- ▸ Lease Worksheet (optional)

The first letter is for approaching a landowner that you've previously approached but has denied you permission. The second letter can be used for a landowner you've never approached before or for a landowner with delinquent taxes. The third letter may be used if you get no response to your first letter. This letter is to be used if the land is really hot and you are very interested in obtaining permission to hunt on it. I would send the second letter about six weeks after the first letter is sent. If you didn't send the personal or club profile, references or lease worksheet with the first letter, now may be the time to do that.

Land for Sale – Newspaper Ads

If you don't have a specific property in mind or you have been unsuccessful with a reluctant landowner, you may want to consider seeking permission to hunt on private land that is listed for sale in the newspaper.

This method will probably bring more success if you are willing to pay for hunting privileges in the form of a lease. You may not want to lease hunting land that is for sale if you're looking for long-term hunting privileges even though it could turn into a long-term thing. I have been hunting on some land that has been for sale for six years. Each year I contact the owner and ask his permission to hunt from October to December, and each year he agrees.

Look in the real estate section of newspapers from areas where you would be interested in hunting. Some people have a tract of land they want to sell but are having a hard time selling it. With a large tract of land, the owner is usually asking a hefty price for it and it can take several years for a buyer to come along. The landowner may be interested in making some money by leasing his property while waiting for a buyer to come along.

Take a ride to see the land before you do any more work. It may or may not be suitable for hunting. If you don't have enough information from the newspaper ad to find the property on your own, don't be afraid to call the telephone number listed with the ad and ask for directions. The ad may be placed by a private individual or by a Realtor. In either case, call the telephone number and tell them you saw the ad in the newspaper and would like to drive by the property to see it. You should also take this opportunity to ask for the name of the property owner. You could do this by asking if their are any "POSTED" signs with their name on it to mark the property that would help you to determine that you have found the right property. You may or may not get the owner's name, but having that information could save you a lot of time in the future. You don't have to give your name or phone number. Just say that if you like the property, you will call back. Keep a record of the person you spoke with and when. You'll use this in your introduction letter.

If you find the property interesting and wish to pursue permission to hunt, it's time to contact the property owner or the Realtor with a letter. If you don't already know the name of the owner, you can follow the steps in Chapter 1; Records Office. You want to be up front with the landowner – your intent is to ask for permission to hunt on the land.

Sample letters that can be used to send to a private individual or Realtor are in the Appendix at the back of the guide. Remember, correct spelling and a professional appearance are essential. The letter and envelope should be neatly typed and your return address should appear on both the letter and the envelope.

The letter to the private landowner should explain that you saw the land advertised in the newspaper and whether you spoke to him by telephone on a specific date to ask for directions. You should be clear that you are proposing to lease the land for hunting privileges for a specific period of time. The letter must be written in a convincing fashion and explain that you are proposing a win-win situation where the landowner can continue to keep his land for sale while making some money on it at the same time.

You may also consider including the following information with the introduction letter:

- ▸ Personal or club profile
- ▸ References
- ▸ Lease Worksheet

When sending a letter to a Realtor, keep in mind that there are some Realtors who specialize in selling farms and large tracts of land. The letter should explain who you are and that you are seeking to lease land for hunting purposes. The letter should be written in a professional manner and explain that you are proposing a situation where all parties can benefit. Don't include a lease worksheet when sending a letter to a Realtor. The Realtor probably has experience with leases and may offer to draw up the leasing documents.

Bulletin Boards

Placing ads on bulletin boards can be a very useful tool when trying to locate a landowner who is willing to lease his property for hunting. By placing ads in strategic places, you will attract a variety of landowners.

Some of the most popular places to post ads are supermarkets, diners, gas stations, hardware stores and convenience stores. All types of people visit these businesses and some of them may own huntable property.

You may also want to target the type of person that you KNOW owns huntable land, such as a farmer. Some good places to put a bulletin board ad that a farmer will see are farming supply stores, tractor dealerships and repair stores, grain and feed mills, farming associations, or farm co-op centers.

The idea is to put an attractive, professional looking sign at a location where people who own a large parcel of property may frequent. The ad is easy. You can use the example in the Appendix to help you with ideas.

Before making the ad, here are some things to consider:

> Include Who, What, Why, Where, When and How. For instance;
> > Who: Small group of responsible hunters
> > What: Seeking land to lease
> > Why: For hunting
> > Where: In Monroe County
> > When: For 1999 deer season (November – December)
> > How: Call 321-555-5678 for more information

> The ad should be attractively typed or printed on white paper and glued to a colorful posterboard that provides a border around all of the edges. This will make your ad stand out and look professional.

> Put your phone number on some kind of card or tear-off strips to make it as easy as possible for the person interested in your ad to call you.

> Don't crowd the ad with too much information. Make it clear and simple to read.

> The next time you go to a supermarket or diner, look for a bulletin board and take note of what attracts your attention to a particular ad. Whether the ad is for a used bicycle or free kittens, there will be certain things about the appearance of the ad that catch your eye and make you want to read it.

> The size of the ad is important. Take note of the size of the bulletin board where you plan to put your ad before you design it. Have some courtesy and leave room for other people. If the ad is too big, the owner of the establishment may take it down or other people are just going to pin their

business cards and garage sale announcements over your ad. On the other hand, if the bulletin board is large, make sure your ad is big enough to get noticed.

▸ Ask the person who owns the establishment or a manager for permission to place the ad on the bulletin board. They will probably say "yes". Also, if they know it is there and what it's about, they may know someone who would be interested. This can be especially helpful in farm supply stores and grain and feed mills where the clerk and the patron might know each other on a more personal level.

You should also be aware that there are people who don't agree with hunting and it is possible that your ad may be defaced. You should check your ad from time to time to make sure another ad isn't covering it or to replace it with a new one.

When is a good time to place an ad on a bulletin board? Well, anytime is good, but there are some times that are better. One time that comes to mind, as I mentioned before, is tax time. This could be income tax, school tax, or property tax time. Anytime to attract attention and get a positive response is when people have money on their minds. You could start your ad by boldly printing, *"Need help paying your property taxes?"*

Be prepared for when a landowner calls you. Here is a list of the things you may need:

▸ Letter to send the landowner
▸ Lease Worksheet
▸ References
▸ Personal or club profile

Some things you may want to ask are:

▸ How much property does the landowner own?
▸ Describe it. Is it wooded, mixed with fields?
▸ Do the fields have crops planted in them?
▸ Do other people hunt on the property?
▸ Has the landowner seen many deer (or other game) on the property?
▸ Can a meeting be arranged with the landowner to see the property?

If the property owner wants details about how much you're going to pay him, tell him that details can be discussed after you see the property. You wouldn't want to give too many details over the phone until you are sure you are talking with the landowner. I suggest approaching each caller with a certain amount of caution and be aware of pranksters. The caller could be some other hunter trying to find out how much you're willing to pay or it could be some scam artist impersonating a property owner and scamming you for the money. Follow Chapter 7 on leases before signing anything.

Ask politely when would be a convenient time to meet with him, see the property and discuss the rest of the details. Fine points like terms and conditions of the lease and money are best discussed in person anyway. You may also want to verify the information at the courthouse to make sure the person you are meeting with is, in fact, the property owner before you sign any lease or hand over any money.

When using bulletin boards to locate landowners, don't expect instant results. Not everybody who goes into a place of business looks at the bulletin boards. It may take some time to get noticed and you may have to replace a couple of signs, but it's a cheap and effective way to let people know that you or your club are looking for property to lease for hunting.

CHAPTER 4

GOOD REASONS TO GRANT PERMISSION

This chapter provides information that could be extra ammunition for getting permission. For instance, before talking with a landowner you should arm yourself with positive hunting facts and the negative effects of NOT helping to control the deer population.

Consider bringing up the subject of crop damage when approaching a farmer. You can find articles in newspapers and farming magazines where research has been done to prove that farmers lose a percentage of their crops due to deer damage. You may find information that puts a dollar amount on the loss that deer are responsible for.

Deer can also do damage to expensive landscaping, shrubbery and gardens. In some areas, if you don't put a fence around your garden you won't have anything to harvest because the deer will eat it all first. Some people in my neighborhood put small fences around their shrubbery to keep deer from eating it. Those who don't fence in their shrubs have landscaping that is eaten from the ground up. Many flowers don't exist in my neighborhood, particularly tulips, as these are a special treat for deer to eat.

What about deer ticks? There is a lot of information in libraries and magazines, especially outdoor magazines, which give scientific facts about deer ticks and Lyme Disease. This may not interest a farmer but would certainly be important to private landowners. For example, deer ticks are found in abundance in many states. Residents risk being bitten by a deer tick and infected with Lyme Disease just by going out in their backyard, let alone venturing out into the woods. People fear the threat of Lyme Disease to themselves, their children and their pets. Find out what the statistics are in your area regarding deer ticks and Lyme Disease and be ready to discuss them with the landowner.

More and more information is becoming available about damage to vehicles, insurance costs, injuries and deaths related to collisions with deer on the roadways. What are the statistics in your area? If you're seeking permission on a specific property because you suspect there are a lot of deer residing there, chances are that the landowner has had more than one encounter with a deer on the road. This is something he will be able to relate to and may encourage him to grant you permission to hunt.

Look for information about the effects of deer overpopulation. You can often appeal to non-hunters by showing them that you actually care about the deer and that you're not just out to kill them. Learn about the effects of starvation after a long winter and how the deer suffer. Find out about the genetic defects and diseases that deer inherit from interbreeding. You can probably find pictures that show these results. It's true that a picture speaks a thousand words. Use these pictures with caution and know what you're talking about.

By casually bringing up one or more of these subjects while speaking with the landowner, you could greatly improve your chances of getting permission to hunt on his property.

CHAPTER 5

NURTURING THE RELATIONSHIP

Once you have permission, don't forget to give something back. Whether you plan on getting permission to hunt again, you should show your appreciation for the privileges you've enjoyed.

A simple Christmas card after the hunting season or a polite Thank You note may be all it takes to ensure yourself a spot for next year. Think twice about sharing pictures of the deer hanging from its neck with its tongue hanging out. Save them for your scrapbook.

After the hunting season, you might want to stop in or call the landowner and tell him you are going to do some scouting for next season. You might want to go on and say how you're interested in how the deer are doing this time of year – what their travel patterns are, what they are eating, etc. This can serve three purposes:

1. You will establish that you are not only nuts for walking around in the woods in the bitter cold, but you are very interested and serious about your sport. The landowner will probably respect that you are not just a deerslayer; you're a serious sportsman.
2. It may be several weeks after the hunting season and the landowner will still remember the nice Thank You card or Christmas card you sent him and his family. This will implant another positive impression of you.
3. We can all use a little more time in the woods to make plans for next year.

The following is a list of things that you could do if this property you now have permission to hunt on is really nice and you want to continue hunting there in the future. Keep in mind that these things may not be necessary. I just look at them as the icing on the cake; a way to seal the deal and begin a lasting friendship:

▸ Offer vegetables from your garden
▸ Offer homemade baked goods
▸ Send a Christmas card
▸ Send a Thank You card

▸ Send a giftbasket
▸ Drop off a couple of deer steaks and a bottle of wine
▸ Drop off a gift certificate for dinner at a nice, local restaurant

If you have professional skills such as carpentry, plumbing or electrical experience, you might consider offering your services if the opportunity arises. A Saturday's work helping around the property can go a long way in assuring that you'll be welcome in the future. Just make sure that you actually know how to do the work and finish the job. You don't need the landowner's house to catch fire or his truck to break down because of something you did...a sure sign the welcome mat will be pulled next season.

The idea is to nurture the hunter-landowner relationship throughout the year, not just during the hunting season. A small gesture of kindness and friendship can go a long way to ensure you are welcomed on the landowner's property again.

CHAPTER 6

REJECTION

This is a section that I really didn't want to write. However, I felt compelled to complete my mission of providing you with as much information as possible to encourage hunter-landowner relations and preserve that relationship for future generations.

If you do not obtain permission, by all means, don't act rudely toward the landowner. Politely tell him that you understand and thank him for his time. If possible, use this opportunity to ask why he decided against granting you permission. Take note of his reason(s). Perhaps you may contact this landowner again in the future and you will know exactly what he liked or disliked about your proposal. You may also learn what you could do differently when contacting another landowner. Evaluate the rejection the same way you would a day you spent bow hunting and consistently spotted deer 10 yards out of your range. What could you have done differently to make that day a success?

You will also find that some landowners simply will not grant permission no matter what you do or say. You have to keep in mind that even after all of your hard work and research, you are asking for a favor. It is his property which he works very hard for. He has every right to say who can come on the property and who can not.

The worst thing you can do is to make the landowner upset with your reaction to his rejection. Not only will you ruin it for yourself, but also you will ruin it for anyone else. If you leave a bad impression, he may tell everyone he knows about the experience. You will develop a bad reputation with the community. That bad reputation could have a negative effect on other hunters.

Keep it simple. If you get rejected, take it in stride and move on to the next piece of property.

CHAPTER 7

LEASES

It's sad but true. Leasing land for hunting is becoming as common as paying to put air in your tires at a gas station. With increased land development and the cost of owning property like taxes and insurance, it's easy to understand why hunters are being squeezed onto smaller pieces of property and the right to hunt on that property has become a hot commodity. I'm not saying that the only way to get permission to hunt on private property is to pay for it. I am saying that if you find it difficult to get permission, you may want to consider forming a small club with your friends and offer money to a landowner for the privilege of hunting on that property.

By definition, a lease is a contract by which one party gives to another the use of land for a specified time and for fixed payments.

For our purpose, it's really quite simple. You give a landowner money in exchange for his permission to allow you to hunt on his property. But before running out with cash in your hand, there are some things to consider before writing a lease:

> ▸ Does the person you are signing the lease with actually own the property? The person may lease it himself for farming or be the caretaker of the property. Be sure the person you deal with has the authority to grant permission.

> ▸ Because laws may vary from state to state, I strongly recommend seeking legal advice with an attorney before attempting to write a lease on your own.

> ▸ In order to help the attorney and to keep your costs down, you may want to use the lease worksheet provided in the Appendix.

> ▸ For the most part, leases pertaining to hunting privileges are primarily set up to protect the landowner and his property from liability and damages. The hunting party's interests may include type of game, treestands, price and sole rights.

▸ Have an attorney already contacted with basic information about your intentions. It is also good to know which attorney you are using in case you are asked by the landowner. It will show that you are serious and on the ball. This will also give you the opportunity to ask the attorney about the cost of drawing up or reviewing a lease.

▸ Be sure to have two copies of your lease worksheet so when you are going over the worksheet with the landowner he can have a copy to read for himself. This indicates that you are organized and shows consideration for the landowner as well. These two copies should also be signed for each of you to keep.

▸ Have all the information that you already know filled in. Again, this will show the landowner that you are organized and considerate not to take any more time than needed to fill out the worksheet.

▸ If money wasn't discussed previously, now is the time. Know what you or your club is willing to pay.

▸ Be prepared to politely and thoroughly explain any part of the lease worksheet to the landowner, if asked.

▸ If you get the feeling the landowner is a little hesitant with the legality of a lease and might back out of the deal, offer to have your attorney explain the lease to him after it is written (check with your attorney for the cost of this first).

▸ Make it clear what season(s) you will hunt (bow, rifle...). Some landowners will only allow hunting during certain seasons. Also, make it clear what game you will hunt. Some landowners will only allow you to hunt antlerless deer on their property.

▸ Discuss with the club members the possibility of acquiring hunter's insurance. Hunter's insurance is discussed in Chapter 8.

▸ When filling out the "Leased Property Description," be specific. For example, "Approximately 580 acres situated on Mountain Road, Monroe County, Pennsylvania," OR, "Approximately 580 acres of land known as the Johnson Ranch, shown highlighted in red on the map attached to this lease."

▸ Will you, the lessee, be required to pay a security deposit to hold the property and to insure your faithful performance of the lease?

▸ Treestands – The landowner may not like you pounding nails into his trees. I suggest you make the statement that if treestands will be used, they will be of the chain-on, ladder or climbing type so as not to injure the trees.

▸ Parking – the landowner may not appreciate you pulling up to his house at 5:00 a.m. and making his dogs bark. You should agree on designated parking area(s) with the landowner.

Lease Worksheet

The guidelines found in the Appendix will help you to fill out a lease worksheet. By completing this worksheet with the landowner you can save time and money. This will avoid passing papers back and forth while making changes to please both parties (usually to please the landowner).

A rough draft of a lease made by yourself may or may not be considered a legal, binding agreement in your state unless reviewed and approved by an attorney. Whatever the case, it will probably only cost $25 or $50 to have an attorney draw up an official lease with all those fancy phrases and words known as legalese. That's a small price to pay for peace of mind.

CHAPTER 8

INSURANCE

You're trying to obtain permission to hunt on private property. You might say, "Why do I need insurance? I've hunted on other property and no one asked me for insurance!"

You owe it to yourself and the property owner to look into some form of liability insurance. You may be able to get permission to hunt the property you're interested in without insurance, but you can increase your chances with it. This will show the landowner that you are serious and will act in a safe and responsible manner.

Let's look at the situation with the eyes of the landowner. He only knows you from your letter and a 20-minute conversation on his porch. You can't blame the property owner for being hesitant to grant you permission. Think about what you're going to be doing. You're asking for permission to walk around on his property with some type of firearm and possibly strap yourself 16 feet up into a tree. There is a lot of room for error.

There are many insurance agencies with a variety of different coverage's, rates and policies. The problem is they are not all geared to cover hunters and hunting clubs. There are some, however, that do cover sportsmen's clubs, though many of these coverage's are specially designed for private, nonprofit organizations with controlled memberships. You may say, "I don't have a club. It's just my son and me or my friend". Get a couple of buddies and form a club; if for no other reason than to fulfill the requirements of the insurance agencies.

There are many things an insurance policy can offer. The following is a list of some of the coverage's they can provide:

- ▶ Landowner coverage – this covers the landowner for bodily injury and property damage. It protects the landowner from damages caused by someone from the club who is hunting on the property.

- ▶ Medical coverage – will pay medical costs in case someone gets hurt during the act of hunting.

- ▶ Emergency Medical Transportation – will pay for transportation to a hospital in case someone gets hurt during the act of hunting.

‣ Treestand coverage – provides for bodily injury and property damage for treestand-related claims.

Requirements of Insurance Companies

Most insurance companies require members to be affiliated with organizations having recognized training and safety programs like the National Rifle Association or National Bowhunters Association. In Pennsylvania, hunters are required to take a hunters' safety course prior to obtaining a hunting license. It is a good idea to have club members attend a similar safety course every two years or so.

Premiums for insurance coverage will vary from one company to another, but you can expect to pay $200 to $600 dollars a year depending on the amount of protection and the various options you may want to include. For instance, coverage for treestands tends to increase the premium.

Hunting insurance is obviously not a requirement but is an option that can work in your favor to successfully gain permission to hunt on private property.

CHAPTER 9

HUNTING CLUBS

If you're having a hard time getting permission to hunt on private property, you might consider starting a hunting club. There are several reasons why you may want to consider this option.

First, leasing land is gaining popularity between hunters and landowners. For the average hunter, it is probably impractical to lease land as an individual because of the cost. It would be more practical to share the cost with other people who have the same interest. A small group of hunters may enable you to generate the money necessary for leasing property.

Second, a hunting club can provide you with more credibility in the mind of a landowner. A landowner will look at a well-organized group of hunters more seriously than three guys that pulled into his driveway without having thought it through.

Next, hunting clubs all over the country help to support the larger national organizations such as the National Rifle Association or the National Bow Hunters Association through their affiliations with them. This support gives all hunters a louder voice in the political forum through their membership.

Furthermore is the intangible, personal benefit that a hunting club can cultivate. You will be sharing your interest and experiences about hunting with the other members that creates lasting friendships. If you or the other members of the club have children, the club will provide an opportunity for families to pass on a responsible hunting tradition to future generations.

In addition to these numerous benefits, there are other reasons to start a hunting club. Acquiring hunting insurance will show the landowner that you and your hunting club are responsible and serious. Before purchasing insurance, you have to meet the policy requirements. Most insurance companies who work with hunters require them to be affiliated with one of the many national organizations like the National Rifle Association. Most of these national organizations require the hunter to be a member of a hunting organization or club consisting of at least five members.

A hunting club can be formed with as little as three people, or it can be more complex with more people, including a president, vice president, secretary, treasurer, club grounds, fund-raising, etc. Most national organizations require you to have a membership organization consisting of at least five members to meet their requirements for affiliation.

When looking for people to join your club, you will want to find people who have some compatibility. You will need people who can agree on things and uphold the rules set up by the club and the landowner. There is nothing that can spoil a good thing more quickly than someone breaking the rules and upsetting the landowner. Look for club members who:

> ▸ can commit the money to lease land and/or purchase insurance
> ▸ are law abiding
> ▸ are trustworthy
> ▸ are respectful
> ▸ are safe hunters

Your club should set up some guidelines, rules and objectives. It may be worth writing some of these down and have everyone in the club read, understand and sign their name to them. For example:

Club Rules

> ▸ I will consider myself a guest on the landowner's property and conduct myself accordingly.
> ▸ I have recently taken a hunter's safety course and I will obey the rules of safe firearm handling.
> ▸ I will obey all state game laws and regulations.
> ▸ I will do my best to assure clean, sportsmanlike harvests.

Club Objectives

> ▸ To strengthen landowner-hunter relations
> ▸ To promote hunter safety
> ▸ To promote wildlife conservation

If you decide to form a hunting club, it's important for your club to have a favorable image in the eyes of the community. There are several ways this can be accomplished. Are any of the club's members part of the local ambulance crew or volunteer fire department? Can your club help to raise money for a common, local cause such as new playground equipment by selling raffle tickets? Does your club donate food (game or canned goods) to organizations such as Hunters Feeding the Hungry? A larger club may have the capacity to help sponsor sporting events for kids by making a donation or even supplying uniforms with the club's name on them.

Community events are also a good way to expose your club to the public. Your club could set up a food or game stand at the county fair, which is a good place to meet private individuals, farmers or local business owners. Perhaps your community holds functions such as the Special Olympics. Your club could consider being a sponsor of such an event. If you are seeking permission to hunt on the property of a specific business, find out what community events the business participates in. Your club could also be part of the event. This is a good opportunity to network and to meet some of the people in the business. If your club can afford it, it will bring some common ground between your club and the people you are trying to get permission to hunt from.

The above-mentioned activities and affiliations can be included in the hunting club's profile. They can help convince a landowner that your club's members are responsible, good people and not gun-toting, burly men stomping through the woods killing helpless animals.

The club profile is like a résumé for the hunting club. It helps the landowner get to know a little about the club and its members before actually meeting them. The club profile should be sent in addition to a letter that the club would send to a landowner to request permission to hunt. The club profile provides the club with a way to communicate their credentials in a convincing and organized fashion. In the Appendix you will find an example of a club profile that you can use as a guideline to set one up for your own hunting club.

As you can see, a hunting club serves many purposes in your pursuit of permission to hunt on private property. It will help to raise the needed money for leasing. It adds credibility to your request. A group of people is usually necessary to fulfill the requirements for hunter's insurance. All hunting clubs, whether large or small, help to support all hunters through their affiliations with national organizations. But in addition to these things, a hunting club provides camaraderie and a place to bring family members together to share in the tradition and heritage of hunting, which will promote the sport for future generations.

CONCLUSION

I want to take this opportunity to thank you for purchasing this guide. I hope you found it informative and helpful and I wish you every success in obtaining permission to hunt on private property.

This guide has taken you from identifying the property you are targeting to learning about both the owner and the land through various resources. The guide has provided numerous strategies to use in approaching farmers, private landowners and businesses. It has described methods of attracting landowners to the idea of leasing their property to hunters and has given you a starting point for developing a lease of your own. This guide has also supplied information about insurance, hunting clubs and sustaining the hunter-landowner relationship.

There is no guarantee that all of these ideas will work every time you try them. However, if you apply the information with the same planning, persistence and patience that you use when you set out on your hunting adventures, you will enhance your chances of success.

I also want to congratulate you on doing your part to ensure that the sport of hunting will continue to be an American tradition. It is the responsibility of all hunters to preserve and promote the tradition of all forms of hunting: to share the experience of hunting with family and friends and to create lifelong memories of wholesome adventures in the great outdoors; to respect not only the game all hunters pursue, but the land that we and the animals live on; and to respect landowners so that the great tradition of hunting may be passed down to future generations.

Brian Guerro

APPENDIX

Brian Guerro

APPENDIX A

LETTER TO FARMER OR PRIVATE INDIVIDUAL (Not for Leasing)

Buck Hunter
123 Green St.
Anytown, PA 12345
(321) 555-1234

June 1, 1999

Mr. Landowner
456 Brown St.
Anytown, PA 12345

Dear Mr. Landowner:

Perhaps individuals you've never met have stood on your doorstep asking for permission to hunt on your property. You may have felt uncomfortable or were too busy to talk to those individuals.

That is why I'm sending you this letter. I am a ___-year-old husband and father who has worked for XYZ Company in Sometown, PA for ___ years. I have lived in Anytown, PA for ___ years, and I enjoy outdoor activities with my family and friends. I have included a personal profile that describes a little bit more about myself.

I would like to respectfully ask your permission for hunting privileges during the _____ *(insert specific hunting season or year)* season. I think of myself as a responsible, ethical outdoorsman. I would consider myself a guest on your property and would abide by your rules.

Please fill out the enclosed postage-paid reply slip or feel free to call me collect at your earliest convenience. My phone number is listed above.

Thank you for your time and consideration.

Sincerely,

Buck Hunter

APPENDIX B

LETTER TO FARMER OR PRIVATE INDIVIDUAL (Leasing)

Buck Hunter
123 Green St.
Anytown, PA 12345
(321) 555-1234

June 1, 1999

Mr. Landowner
456 Brown St.
Anytown, PA 12345

Dear Mr. Landowner:

Please allow me to introduce myself. My name is Buck Hunter. I represent the Blue Mountain Hunting Club (or a small group of hunters). We would be very pleased to lease your property during the next _____ *(insert specific hunting season or year)* season. Would you consider leasing your property for hunting purposes?

I have enclosed a profile of Blue Mountain Hunting Club and its members (or Personal Profiles of the individuals in the group). I have also included a postage-paid reply slip for your convenience.

Blue Mountain Hunting Club (or our group) is committed to promoting and preserving the tradition of responsible hunting. Our members are ethical, law-abiding hunters and would consider ourselves guests on your property.

We appreciate your time and consideration. Please feel free to contact me at the above number if you have any questions.

Thank you for your time and consideration.

Sincerely,

Buck Hunter
Blue Mountain Hunting Club

APPENDIX C

REPLY SLIP

APPENDIX D

CONTACTING A COMPANY (Leasing)

Buck Hunter
123 Green St.
Anytown, PA 12345
(321) 555-1234

June 1, 1999

Mr. Corporation
ABC Corporation
456 Brown St.
Anytown, PA 12345

Dear Mr. Corporation:

Please allow me to introduce myself. My name is Buck Hunter. I am the President of Blue Mountain Hunting Club. We would be very pleased to lease ABC Corporation's wooded property during the next _____ *(insert specific hunting season or year)* season. Would you consider leasing your property for hunting purposes?

I have enclosed a profile of Blue Mountain Hunting Club and its members for your review. In summary:

- We are an organized, insured, nonprofit club
- Leasing arrangements will be tailored to meet ABC Corporation's needs
- Payment may be made according to ABC Corporation's direction
- We would willingly pay attorney's fees for the drafting of any relevant paperwork

Blue Mountain Hunting Club is committed to promoting and preserving the tradition of responsible hunting. Our members are ethical, law-abiding hunters and would consider ourselves guests on ABC Corporation's property.

We appreciate your time and consideration. Please feel free to contact me at the above number if you have any questions or simply return the postage-paid reply slip.

Sincerely,

Buck Hunter
President
Blue Mountain Hunting Club

APPENDIX E

TAX TIME – RELUCTANT LANDOWNER WHO HAS DENIED PERMISSION IN THE PAST

Buck Hunter
123 Green St.
Anytown, PA 12345
(321) 555-1234

July 1, 1999

Mr. Landowner
456 Brown St.
Anytown, PA 12345

Dear Mr. / Mrs. Landowner:

You may recall (*speaking with / meeting with / receiving a letter from*) me on or around June 1, 1999. I introduced myself as Buck Hunter, President of the Blue Mountain Hunting Club and indicated our desire to hunt on your property during the _____ (*insert specific season or year*).

We are still very interested in hunting on your land and have discovered a way that we can all benefit. As you are aware, it is tax time again. Blue Mountain Hunting Club would be happy to help pay your taxes by paying for hunting privileges during the _____ (*insert specific season or year*) in the form of a lease.

If this idea appeals to you, please fill out the enclosed reply slip and return it to me in the postage-paid envelope or you may call me at the above telephone number.

We have a standardized lease worksheet that you can review and we can fill out together. Or, if you prefer, we would be happy to retain an attorney to draft the necessary paperwork.

Mr. Landowner, Blue Mountain Hunting Club is serious about leasing your property. We hope you will consider our proposal.

Thank you for your time.

Buck Hunter
President
Blue Mountain Hunting Club

APPENDIX F

TAX TIME – NEW LANDOWNER and/or LANDOWNER WITH DELINQUENT TAXES

Buck Hunter
123 Green St.
Anytown, PA 12345
(321) 555-1234

July 1, 1999

Mr. Landowner
456 Brown St.
Anytown, PA 12345

Dear Mr. / Mrs. Landowner:

It's tax time again. I know how it feels to get that tax notice in the mail. Taxes keep going up and you detest paying them.

But I may be able to offer you a solution. I am the President of the Blue Mountain Hunting Club. We are an organized nonprofit club seeking to lease property for hunting purposes. As club President, I would like to respectfully ask your permission for hunting privileges during the _____ *(insert specific season or year)* season.

Please be assured that the Blue Mountain Hunting Club is committed to promoting and preserving the tradition of responsible hunting. Our members are ethical, law-abiding hunters who would behave as honored guests on your property and would abide by your rules. I have enclosed a profile of our club and its members for your review.

We appreciate your time and consideration. Please feel free to contact me at the above number if you have any questions. You can also return the reply slip in the postage paid envelope at your convenience.

Sincerely,

Buck Hunter
President
Blue Mountain Hunting Club

APPENDIX G

TAX TIME – FOLLOW-UP LETTER

Buck Hunter
123 Green St.
Anytown, PA 12345
(321) 555-1234

July 1, 1999

Mr. Landowner
456 Brown St.
Anytown, PA 12345

Dear Mr. / Mrs. Landowner:

You may recall receiving a letter from me on or around June 1, 1999. In that letter I introduced myself to you as the President of the Blue Mountain Hunting Club and indicated our desire to lease property for the purpose of hunting _____ *(insert game/season).*

Since I can appreciate that you are a busy person, I wanted to follow-up with more information about our club. This information may assist you in making a decision whether to grant us hunting privileges.

- Addresses and informative backgrounds are available describing each of our members
- We can provide our insurance information
- We have a standardized lease worksheet available, or we would be happy to retain an attorney to draft the necessary paperwork
- A postage-paid reply slip is enclosed for your convenience

Mr. Landowner, Blue Mountain Hunting Club is serious about leasing your property. I hope the enclosed information is helpful in getting to know us better.

Thank you for your time.

Buck Hunter
President
Blue Mountain Hunting Club

APPENDIX H

LAND FOR SALE – PRIVATE OWNER

Buck Hunter
123 Green St.
Anytown, PA 12345
(321) 555-5678

June 1, 1999

Mr. Landowner
456 Brown St.
Anytown, PA 12345

Dear Mr. Landowner:

I am writing to you in reference to the land you have advertised for sale in the Daily News.

I represent the Blue Mountain Hunting Club (or a small group of responsible hunters) who are interested in leasing your property for _____ *(insert specific season or year)* season.

I understand that you wish to sell the property, but I am proposing a win-win situation where you can continue to keep the property for sale while making some extra money while leasing it to us.

I am enclosing a lease worksheet with some of the items we are interested in already completed and a club (or personal) profile. I want to make certain that you understand this is a proposal and the terms of the lease can be negotiated.

Please take the time to review this information and feel free to contact me at the address or telephone number listed above. Once again, I would like to thank you for your time and look forward to hearing from you in the near future.

Sincerely,

Buck Hunter
President
Blue Mountain Hunting Club

<u>APPENDIX I</u>

LAND FOR SALE – REALTOR

Buck Hunter
123 Green St.
Anytown, PA 12345
(321) 555-5678

June 1, 1999

Mr. Realtor
456 Brown St.
Anytown, PA 12345

Dear Mr. Realtor:

Please allow me to introduce myself. My name is Buck Hunter. I represent Blue Mountain Hunting Club. It is my understanding that you specialize in selling large tracts of land. Our club is currently looking for a large tract of land to lease for hunting.

I understand that your clients are interested in selling their property. However, I am proposing a win-win situation where all parties could benefit by leasing the land to us while it remains on the market. Our club is flexible and will consider leasing for a short-term or a long-term period.

I have included a club profile that provides information about our club and its members. If you or your clients have any questions, please feel free to contact me at the address or telephone number listed above.

I want to thank you for your time and look forward to hearing from you.

Sincerely,

Buck Hunter
President
Blue Mountain Hunting Club

<u>APPENDIX J</u>

LETTER FOR BULLETIN BOARD ADS

Buck Hunter
123 Green St.
Anytown, PA 12345
(321) 555-5678

June 1, 1999

Mr. Landowner
456 Brown St.
Anytown, PA 12345

Dear Mr. Landowner:
    I am writing to you in reference to our phone conversation on _____ *(insert date)*. During that conversation you indicated that you were interested in leasing your property to Blue Mountain Hunting Club for the purpose of hunting.
    As we discussed on the phone, I am enclosing a club profile and a lease worksheet for your review.
    I would like the opportunity to meet with you so we can discuss the terms of the agreement in more detail.
    Once again, I would like to thank you for your time and look forward to speaking with you. I will call you on _____ *(insert date)* to arrange a convenient time to meet with you.

    Sincerely,

    Buck Hunter
    President
    Blue Mountain Hunting Club

APPENDIX K

EXAMPLES OF BULLETIN BOARD ADS

(Who)	**SMALL GROUP OF HUNTERS**
(What)	**SEEKING LAND TO LEASE**
(Why)	**FOR HUNTING**
(Where)	**IN MONROE COUNTY, PENNSYLVANIA**
(When)	**FOR 1999 DEER SEASON**
(How)	**CALL FOR INFORMATION**

ATTENTION LANDOWNERS
**Let us help pay your property taxes
Small group of hunters looking
For property to lease for hunting
Insured, Responsible**

APPENDIX L

LEASE WORKSHEET

1) Date lease is made.

   _____

2) Complete name and address of Lessor (landowner).

   _____

   _____

   _____

3) Complete name and address of Lessee (hunter).

   _____

   _____

   _____

4) Leased Property Description

   _____

   _____

   _____

5) Duration of lease:
   The first day of the Lease is _____ and the last day of the Lease is _____.

6) Rent for the Lease is:
   ▷ $_____ for the entire season / month (circle one) due on
   _____

   ▷ OR   describe   customized   arrangement:
   _____

   _____

   _____

7) Security Deposit
   ▷ None
   ▷ Yes, Lessee shall pay a security deposit of $ _____.

8) Use of leased property:
   What season(s) will be hunted:
   ▷ Bow and arrow
   ▷ Rifle
   ▷ Shotgun

▷ Muzzleloader
▷ Other _____

What game will be hunted:
▷ Antlered whitetail deer
▷ Antlerless whitetail deer
▷ Turkey
▷ Bear
▷ Other _____

Other use of land:
▷ Fishing
▷ Camping
▷ Scouting/Hiking
▷ Target Practice
▷ Other _____

9) Parties allowed to hunt:
  ▷ Those persons specifically named in the Exhibit named "Club Members" attached to the Lease.
  ▷ Those persons specifically named in the Exhibit named "Club Members" and guests. Number of guests not to exceed _____ per club member.

10) Insurance
  ▷ Not required.
  ▷ Yes, with limits of $_____ for bodily injury and $_____ for property damage.

11) Treestands
  ▷ May be used and will be of chain-on, ladder or climbing type.
  ▷ May not be used.

12) Following are some general statements that you may want to consider including in your lease:

  ▷ Property owner will not be responsible to any member of the hunting group for any personal injury, death or property damage which shall be sustained or inflicted by any party as a result of Lessee's use of the premises.

  ▷ It is understood that everyone in the hunting group will abide by all state game laws.

▷ Members of the hunting group will park in the designated area(s) described as: _____.

▷ It is understood that no member of the hunting group will construct a fire or use devices with open flames.

▷ No member of the hunting group will remove any minerals, soil, coal, timber or iron from the premises.

▷ Members of the hunting group will not leave trash or waste of any kind, including shell casings on the property.

▷ The property owner understands and agrees that the members of the hunting group will use firearms on the premises and the property owner will advise any visitors to exercise appropriate care, if and when they are on the subject premises.

▷ Club members may post "No Trespassing" and/or "No Hunting" signs on the premises as they shall see fit.

▷ Other information:

_____
_____
_____
_____
_____
_____
_____
_____
_____
_____
_____
_____
_____
_____
_____
_____
_____

APPENDIX M

CLUB PROFILE

Blue Mountain Hunting Club

NAME: Blue Mountain Hunting Club (BMHC)

FOUNDED: 1988

MEMBERS: 4

AFFILIATIONS: National Rifle Association
Pennsylvania Bow Hunters
Hunters Feeding the Hungry

**SUPPORTING
SPONSORSHIPS:**   Morey Township Little League Soccer (girls & boys)
Morey Playground Fund

**MISSION
STATEMENT:**   Our mission is to continually improve hunter-landowner relations and to assure quality open land for future generations.

CLUB RULES:

‣ We consider ourselves as guests on the landowner's property and conduct ourselves accordingly.
‣ We have recently taken a hunter's safety course and we will obey the rules of safe firearm handling.
‣ We will obey all state game laws and regulations.
‣ We will do our best to assure clean, sportsmanlike harvests.

CLUB OBJECTIVES:

‣ To strengthen landowner-hunter relations
‣ To promote hunter safety
‣ To promote wildlife conservation

CLUB PROFILE – Blue Mountain Hunting Club

MEMBER OVERVIEW:

- ▸ Families – ages 15 to 62
- ▸ U.S citizens
- ▸ Have no criminal records
- ▸ All members have passed state hunter safety courses

MEMBER PROFILES: Buck Hunter

- ▸ President of BMHC, 10 years
- ▸ Pennsylvania rifle hunter for 20 years
- ▸ Pennsylvania bow hunter for 14 years
- ▸ Member of Morey Township Volunteer Fire Dept. for 7 years

John Doe

- ▸ Pennsylvania rifle hunter for 25 years
- ▸ New Jersey shotgun hunter for 10 years

Robin Hood Doe

- ▸ Pennsylvania rifle hunter for 3 years
- ▸ Son of John Doe

Johnny Appleseed

- ▸ Pennsylvania rifle hunter for 40 years
- ▸ Pennsylvania muzzleloader hunter for 30 years
- ▸ Working to promote interest in muzzleloader hunting for future generations

NOTES

MONTH	CROP	FRUIT/VEGETABLE	ORCHARD	LIVESTOCK
JANUARY	*BEST TIME*	*BEST TIME*	*BEST TIME*	Milking
FEBRUARY	*BEST TIME*	*BEST TIME*	*BEST TIME*	Milking
MARCH	ALFALFA / GRASSESplowing / planting	Plowing / planting	Pruning	Plowing / plantingMilking
APRIL	ALFALFA / GRASSESplowing / planting	Plowing / planting	PruningSpraying	Plowing / plantingMilking
MAY	CORN / SOYplowing / plantingHAYCutting	Plowing / planting	Spraying	Plowing / plantingMilking
JUNE	HAYCutting *BEST TIME*	Harvesting *BEST TIME*	*BEST TIME*	First hay cuttingChickens hatchingMilking
JULY	WHEATHarvesting	Harvesting		Milking
AUGUST	HAYCutting	Harvesting		Milking
SEPTEMBER	EARLY CORNHarvesting	Harvesting	Harvesting	Harvest silo cornMilking
OCTOBER	CORN / SOYHarvestingWINTER WHEATPlanting *HUNTING SEASON*	*HUNTING SEASON*	Harvesting *HUNTING SEASON*	HarvestingMilking *HUNTING SEASON*
NOVEMBER	CORN / SOYHarvesting *HUNTING SEASON*	*HUNTING SEASON*	*HUNTING SEASON*	Milking *HUNTING SEASON*
DECEMBER	*HUNTING SEASON*	*HUNTING SEASON*	*HUNTING SEASON*	Milking *HUNTING SEASON*